Complete Horoscope

Leo 2021

Monthly astrological forecasts for 2021

TATIANA BORSCH

Translated from Russian by Sonja Swenson-Khalchenia
Translation copyright © Coinflow Limited, Cyprus
AstraArt Books is an imprint of Coinflow limited, Cyprus
Published by Coinflow Limited, Cyprus
For queries please contact: tatianaborsch@yahoo.com

ISBN: 978-9925-579-38-9 (print)
ISBN: 978-9925-579-39-6 (ebook)

Contents

2021 - Birth of a new world 5

2021 Overview for Leo 13

January 15

February 17

March 19

April 21

May 23

June 25

July 27

August 29

September 31

October 33

November 35

December 37

A guide to Zodiac compatibility 39

Love description of Zodiac Signs 47

2021 - Birth of a new world

Based on the events of this year, my 2020 predictions, which were published on my website and in *SWAAY* magazine, are coming true (I write this article in summer 2020). We are bearing witness to an era of change; the world is teetering on the brink, and everything we thought was permanent and unshakable has turned out not to be. What else lies ahead?

It is impossible to separate the events of 2020 and 2021. These are years of major shifts, with an effect on each country, each home, and each individual. 2020's developments will continue in 2021, and there is simply no equivalent in modern history. It's safe to say that mankind has not experienced these kinds of changes in a very long time.

Major astrological events during this period are:

The first conjunction of Saturn and Jupiter in the air element will take place in Aquarius. This extremely significant event will literally take place as 2020 becomes 2021- on December 25, 2020.

This means the dawn of the Age of Aquarius, which almost everyone has heard about.

The Age of Aquarius is very long, lasting 2,160 years. It is determined by the Earth's shift from one axis to another. This transition period from one age to another can last a long time. Many astrologers believe that it will last at least 100 years. The last 20 years have been turbulent-they were vital preparation for the adoption of new rules for a new era.

All of this means that 2020 is the last year of the outgoing Age of Pisces, and 2021 is the first year of the Age of Aquarius.

Shifting eras is always linked with global shocks, crises of civilization, and economic and cultural revolutions, as well as a new perspective on religious teachings. Even the climate usually undergoes major changes.

Summer and autumn 2020, and all of 2021, are clear indicators of that.

The second most important astrological phenomenon is conflict between Saturn and Uranus, which will continue throughout 2021.

Saturn will square Uranus several times in 2021 – we can divide them into the following periods: January-March, May-the first half of July, December 2021-January 2022.

During these periods, we can expect many problems to rear their heads. It is hard to say exactly how this will influence each individual person as part of a general prediction – everything depends on your personal data, though, generally speaking, I can say that we will see the following trends in during these periods of 2021:

I. First of all, we can expect the economic crisis to expand in scope. Many people will lose their jobs, and companies will go bankrupt.

II. In many countries, we will see social breakdown. People will organize strikes and demonstrations, and the overarching theme will be their discontent with authorities and the current order. We will see confrontation between society and power structures.

III. In global hotspots, we may see new deployments of military force or reescalation of conflict.

IV. For individuals, problems that began in 2019 or 2020 will continue, though this time, things may worsen. Remember – a chain is only as strong as its weakest link.

V. The climate may undergo significant changes- flooding and forest fires will cause extensive damage. Large-scale migrations will be the result. In response, governments of countries in a better position may declare states of emergency or deploy troops in order to prevent unwanted migrants from crossing their borders.

VI. This interaction between Saturn and Uranus is indicative of conflict between old and new ways of life, and a difficult, irreconcilable struggle that will be reflected in all areas of life – social, economic, and political.

Saturn carries the energy of restrictions and structure. At the same time, Uranus is the planet of unexpected, revolutionary change (as well as high tech). Conflict between the two planets leads to sharp changes in existing reality. Transitioning to a new world and a new set of rules will lead to conflict.

Interaction between Saturn and Uranus speaks to opposition to both new and old ways of living, and of the rigid, irreconcilable struggle that is reflected in every sphere of life – social, economic, and political. Most peoples' lives will undergo dramatic changes, and they will have to adapt.

Economics and Politics

Saturn will square Uranus throughout 2021, and this will raise difficult questions – it is time for out with the old, in with the new. But replacing an old system with a new one is rarely a peaceful process. That is why the struggle between old and new economic orders will be a feature of 2020 and 2021.

Former economic systems will begin to transform, right before our very eyes, and these processes will go hand in hand with trade wars, political reckoning, and in some cases, armed conflict.

As the global financial crisis further unfolds, we can expect to see a stronger China, and weakened United States. Countries in the Western financial system will suffer greatly, particularly those in the Eurozone, and American political and economic satellites.

From an astrological perspective, the American presidential elections will take place during one of the most challenging periods of 2020. By now, we are used to political scandals every four years when they occur. However, I fear that the 2020 elections will put all others to shame when it comes to political upheaval.

On Election Day and the period leading up to it, Mercury and Mars will be in retrograde, which means that there will be significant incorrect or intentionally twisted information, crowds of protesters, and this will peak the last week before the elections take place, on November 3. Retrograde planets also point toward the opposition party trying to protest the election results, which will translate into large-scale scandal.

Donald Trump may be re-elected for a second term, if Joe Biden is his only opponent. Incriminating information on Biden will come to light in late September or October 2020, when he will simultaneously battle serious health issues. Generally speaking, Biden's horoscope is much weaker than Trump's.

Whoever ends up as President of the United States will have to face a series of problems in 2021- most of all conflict among members of his inner circle.

The horoscope of the United States, which was founded on the day of its Declaration of Independence, on July 04, 1776, in Philadelphia, Pennsylvania, USA, predicts that America's economic and political might will waste away, and this may take place more quickly than we can imagine.

This crisis in the American system will lead to a drop and depreciation in the US dollar in late 2020 or the first quarter of 2021. The US chart suggests that in 2021, the dollar will be replaced as a reserve currency.

As America weakens, it will face growing confrontations with other countries. In 2021, the US will wield less influence on political and economic allies.

There may even be tides of separatism within the States themselves. Even so, I do not think the United States is threatened by the same fate as the USSR – it is unlikely to disintegrate. But it is possible that in late 2020 or early 2021, some states will declare their desire to secede, and even take some decisive steps in that direction, but full secession is not in the cards. Nonetheless, the struggle will be very difficult for America's political elite and society as a whole.

Large-scale social protests and unrest, which we saw in 2019 and 2020 will continue in 2021, though they may become more aggressive in nature.

This does not only apply to the United States. Social activism will grow worldwide. Mottos of the Age of Aquarius are FREEDOM, EQUALITY, and BROTHERHOOD, and they will be brandished in many countries around the world. This time, the conflict will not only be over ethnic or racial issues, but also pit social classes against each other – the rich versus the poor.

During the second half of 2020, and nearly all of 2021, expect an economic crisis that will spare nearly no country around the world. Many will blame their current governments, and brutal confrontations between citizens and the authorities will follow, oppositions will become active, demonstrations will take place, and instability in some countries may go so far as to topple current regimes.

England will also be dragged into financial crisis, and according to its horoscope, the worst period countrywide is likely to begin in December 2020, and last until September 2023. Expect financial problems, changes in the Royal Family (the Queen is likely to leave the throne between December 2020 and July 2021), and also innovative changes to how the country is governed.

There are also indications that in the summer and fall of 2020, a financial crisis is likely in the Russian Federation, and it will continue into 2021.

During this period, President Putin's horoscope contains indications of a systemic crisis, financial shortages, and growing opposition movements. Any leader's horoscope is largely a reflection of the state of his or her country.

Money

All countries will lean more strongly toward virtual currencies and cryptocurrencies, which will be accepted by many countries' governments over the next three to five years. This will make it easier to control cash flow, and with it, all of us.

Our reality will increasingly take place virtually, and professionals in this arena will make up the most sought-after and highly-paid class of workers.

As far as personal finance, the Zodiac sign horoscopes included in my book, "Complete Horoscope 2021" offer more specific information. But generally speaking, during a transition period, it is better to refrain from taking risks, and best to avoid investing your money in get-rich-quick schemes.

What's more, there is a saying "Don't risk your house on a sure thing"- now, that is surprisingly relevant.

Personal life

A crisis is a crisis, but love is an eternal concept. So long as humans exist, they will live and love. 2021 will likely also be a year of major changes in this arena. While tragedy will befall some, others will find happiness.

Unstable partnerships are likely to fall apart, and all the problems faced by unhappy couples are likely to rear their ugly heads.

Unexpected breakups are a possibility, and in many cases, this will be related to an existential crisis, internal discomfort, or maybe even material losses.

Couples with a sincere bond and real affection for one another may be able to take their relationship to the next level, for example, they may begin living together, or get married.

The political, economic, and social shifts underway might force many to move, find a new place to live, or acquire real estate. Many people may also find themselves immersed in issues related to housing- buying or restoring a home, and in some cases, that may be related to moving to another city or even abroad.

In that scenario, be careful and pay attention- due to the conflict between Saturn and Uranus, it is not worth making any investments in a completed construction or second home unless the project has already been proven.

People will begin to seriously reconsider their views on the concept of marriage in the near future. During the Age of Aquarius, bonds between people will be built on ideas of equality and spiritual unity.

The current trend of increasing numbers of non-traditional relationships will only grow stronger.

Differences between the sexes will gradually fade away, as Aquarius is the sign of unisex. Marriage itself will begin to resemble the classic model less and less, as it becomes free, and in some cases, "open". This may bring both advantages and serious disadvantages. Obviously, freedom is a good thing. But that freedom often goes hand in hand with loneliness.

Conflict between Saturn and Uranus will lead to a generational conflict. Saturn represents the older generation, parents, while Uranus represents rebellious children. That means that the younger generation will actively push back against pressure from their elders, and the older generation will need to become wiser and more flexible.

equality & spiritual
unity

Health

Technology will play a greater role in medicine, affecting every branch of it.

The union of Saturn and Jupiter, and their tension toward Uranus suggest unexpected deaths, which may be due to various types of accidents and cataclysms.

Those suffering from chronic cardiovascular or spinal diseases should take special precautions.

We may encounter a "second wave" of coronavirus, or outbreaks of new, unknown diseases.

I entitled this article "Birth of a New World". Birth is a painful process, and a mother's body undergoes significant changes, but the fact remains that birth is a great joy for parents and loved ones. The same can be said for 2021. It will not be an easy year, and many will have a difficult time – whether they face problems at work or in their personal life, but that is the logical continuation of the period we live in. We will gain experience and knowledge, and see the emergence of new technology, which will open a new chapter in human history. I am certain that after a transition period, the Age of Aquarius will be the beginning of a new, wonderful world.

Tatiana Borsch

July 12, 2020

2021 Overview for Leo

You are moving toward the end of a cycle at work, and that is why you're in for another bumpy year. You once had a clear picture of everything, but some of your goals were so difficult to reach, that you are now asking yourself whether it is worth finishing what you started. Only you can answer that question.

Work. You may become heavily dependent on your business partners. That is not always a bad thing, but this is not one of those times.

Entrepreneurs will suddenly discover that their views are radically different than those of their associates, and this will lead to conflict. In some cases, the business will fall apart.

Employees will face stiff competition in 2021. There may be unexpected conflict with their superiors, which will make them question whether they wish to continue working in that organization.

This situation may continue to ebb and flow all year, and in the most difficult situations, the stars recommend turning to friends or your mentors for help.

They are unlikely to be able to fully resolve the problem, but with some effort, they may be able to mitigate it to a degree.

The most difficult months at work may be the second half of January, February, May, and December. Closer to the end of the year, you will have some difficult decisions to make- should you continue what you started? In many cases, the answer will be no.

Money. Financially, things may look unbalanced this year, due to the mounting problems you will have to face.

Things will only improve in 2022, and you'll just have to get through 2021. In any case, you won't end up penniless, you will keep working and you'll still be making some money.

Love and family. You will go through a significant personal renaissance, though it will look differently, depending on your situation in the past.

The eclipses this year will take place in the love sector of your sky, which means that you won't find yourself alone. Single people will find a chance to start something interesting, and it might just be with someone you've known for a long time. Your relationship will move to the next level, based on love and understanding.

For spouses with grudges, their relationship will be different. Things will look tense and critical, so be careful and tread lightly, if you wish to remain together.

Alternatively, a loved one may have a problem, and you will face the difficult task of shouldering their responsibility.

Health. This year, your energy is lagging, though you won't need to worry about getting sick, as long as you follow a daily routine and remember to rest.

The elderly, weak and those suffering from cardiovascular diseases need to be particularly careful and not forget to take any preventive measures.

Significant personal renaissance

January

January will have you making difficult, but potentially life-altering decisions. This involves people you counted on. There are no friends, now – only business, and nothing more!

Work. You've worked hard and are right to expect that your services are respected and appreciated. Right now, you're busy and things are progressing. Though the first half of January promises calm waters, the second half will bring storms involving your associates. You may be driven apart by different visions of how your work should look now or in the future, and who is in charge. As things course forward, you might say that your position is vulnerable, and you'll end up having to give in.

Don't let things boil over into open conflict or confrontation, which is the clear trend. Sit down, negotiate, try to find a workable way to cooperate, and remember that even the worst peace is better than a good fight – especially now.

During the second half of January, employees may see their relationships with management grow complicated, and this may include stiff competition and various types of intrigue. Moving forward, you can predict that problems that begin now will exacerbate in the future, so prepare to defend yourself. Learn to be patient and document everything, if you can.

Money. Though you are putting out fires at work, your money is still coming in. It may be regular, and the largest sums will arrive closer to the end of the month- January 30, 31.

Love and family. Your personal life is going through an interesting, but very difficult period. Single people can expect someone from their past to reappear, and your relationship with this person will require special attention.

Not everyone in your circle will approve of this relationship, particularly your relatives and parents. It is difficult to predict what the outcome will be in each case, but there is cause for concern. Do what you feel you have to, but you may periodically find yourself asking, "is this really what I want?"

Married couples in stable relationships may overcome work issues together, but you may also encounter quarrels and misunderstandings.

Another possibility – those close to you will need your support, and you will have to assist.

Health. This month, you're feeling a bit sluggish, so take care of yourself and avoid getting a cold or viral infection. Keep a healthy lifestyle, don't overeat, and be careful with alcohol. These basic precautions can go a long way in avoiding complications now and down the road.

February

Should you make a concession or fight to the end? The stars recommend the former. Sit down to negotiate, and bargain, one thing at a time.

Work. The trend you're dealing with this February is disagreements with business associates, which may have begun in January, if not earlier.

Just as before, this will stem from differing opinions on the development of your work, and who it belongs to. Your position is not so stable, so lean on friends for support, as well as anyone else up to the task.

Don't rush things – you are unlikely to resolve any of this now, and things look like they can be put off for later.

This of course pertains more to entrepreneurs and managers, while employees may encounter changes in their place of work. That may be due to changes in leadership, new directions, or new people as well.

Many will face stiff competition and unfairness from management. Keep a close eye on your duties, and don't forget the details. Listen more and talk less.

This is not a time where "truth is born in a dispute". When defending your position, stick to the facts, and avoid getting into arguments.

Money. Your finances are likely to be neutral. Competing interests and ideas about money are not yet coming to light.

Love and family. Any unpleasant situations in February most likely involve your job, and problems are likely to bypass your personal life.

The exception to this is couples with shared business, who have already dealt with problems. This month, contradictions may worsen, and in some cases, lead to divorce or a separation of affairs, including real estate.

Health. You may find yourself worrying excessively and stressing this month, which is the most negative thing you can do to your nervous system, which, doctors believe, is the source of all illnesses.

During this challenging time, try to get enough sleep and remember, your health is number one, the rest will follow.

March

You have been fighting hard for a long time, trying to find a safe path. The time has come- you will either leave things as they are, or give up what you have been fighting for. Of course, the latter is rather unlikely.

Work. March is a period of transitions for Leos with jobs. Striving and overwhelming stress are things of the past, and looking ahead, your future is somewhat blurry. You may be determining your own place at work, convincing your adversaries, and, with the help of influential friends, achieving at least a part of your goals, if not all of them.

Employees can count on management being understanding, and decent compensation in case of dismissal.

The most promising time for all relationships is the second half of March, particularly the last ten days. This is when you will see significant shifts that will determine your future.

Money. This month, many Leos can count on money from a business partner, receiving credit, or dividends from a profitable investment.

Outside of work, you can count on assistance from parents, loved ones, and monetary compensation in cases of divorce.

Love and family. March is a rather promising month for your personal life. Stable couples support each other in everything, and those who engaged in a war of words in February can now see that their differences are minor, and they in fact share similar outlooks.

Those who have opted for divorce may discuss major financial issues, as well as their children's future. This time, things will go smoothly, peacefully, and, possibly, favorably.

Health. For most of March, you are feeling a bit tired, perhaps even lethargic, fatigued, and in a difficult emotional state much of the time. The stars recommend taking care of yourself physically, avoiding catching a cold, infection, and living a healthy lifestyle. Additionally, your loved ones are facing real problems and may need your attention and care. If you are driven to the very limit, then at least get enough sleep, which will let you regain your strength, as you'll need a lot of it this month.

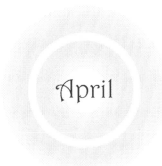

April

Your big win this month is moving ahead and changes. Thanks to that, and shifts in the stars, you can move mountains!

Work. April will have you pushed to your limits, and thanks to your tenacity, you will be able to resolve a number of your previous problems and be successful in your current tasks.

You are seeing your connections with colleagues from other cities or abroad develop, and you might take a trip. You will also see constructive negotiations with partners from far away.

This update will reach every area of your activities, and previous disagreements with adversaries will start to look like they are a thing of the past. This also applies to legal problems.

Despite the favorable trends, during the second half of April, you may once again run into friction with your foes. This time, things won't be as heated and tense, as your position is now stronger, and other, more promising opportunities are on the horizon. All of this may overwhelm your opponents, and their hostility will subside.

Employees will face a real, promising opportunity for a better, more favorable job, or to strengthen their position where they are. Overall, your professional life is stable, and that is definitely a plus.

Money. Your finances are also favorable this month. You are making more, and expect to receive the largest amounts on April 3-5, 13, 14, 22-24.

Love and family. Along with your financial and professional successes, April might also be lucky when it comes to romance. Many Leos will reconnect with old friends, including those who live in other cities or abroad. You may go on a successful trip. Mutual friends might introduce you to someone interesting, and, it's very possible this meeting will be fateful.

All month long, you will sociable, charming, and your friends and colleagues will take note. Wherever you go, you will be received with open arms, and all you need to decide is where, how, and with whom you prefer to spend your time.

Even those who have recently quarreled with their spouse can think of a way to reconcile, and here, your friends, relatives, and children may be a big help. If you do not want to spend your time alone, and you don't want to keep falling into the same trap, this month is the time to discuss some respectable conditions for retreat.

Couples in a stable relationship might go on a trip together, and it will bring you closer together.

Health. This April, you are much more energetic than you were before, and are on the mend from any illnesses you may have experienced last month.

May

You're starting one of the best months of 2021! Some of the decisions you'll have to make now will have major and lasting consequences. Remember to look at the big picture, and you will make the right choices!

Work. This month, you are someone to envy at work. Entrepreneurs and managers will be making decisions about drawing partners' investments in their business, and most of your negotiations on that front will take place in May.

Alternatively, if you have divided your business, your partners might pay you for their share, and you will think about striking out on your own.

Employees are strengthening their position somewhat, and both management and colleagues are supporting you. That may signify a shift in your relationships. This is a good thing, though you will still face competition from a few people.

During the second half of the month, old friends or kindly superiors may play a very important role in everything. Their support is vital, but may be somewhat cumbersome for your bank account.

Money. When it comes to material matters, May is rather looking up. You will receive regular income, and it is significantly more, these days. The first half of May is particularly promising in this arena, when entrepreneurs will be able to count on additional profits, and employees can expect a bonus or severance pay, if they are dismissed.

This month, many Leos will be able to rely on credit, money from business associates, or other sponsorship.

Those who do not work in the business world will also be graced by gifts of financial Fortune. Parents or someone close to you will provide assistance.

Most of your expenses will occur during the second half of the month, and what you need to spend on will depend on each individual person.

Love and family. Your personal life is rather lively, these days. Stable couples might think about starting a family, or maybe buying a new home, too. For now, everything is in the planning phase, but they will start to take shape in the near future.

Couples whose marriages are on the rocks will take a step closer to divorce, and, most likely, dividing up their household.

During the second half of May, you might see old friends and former lovers, it is very likely that you will rekindle a relationship.

Health. This month, you are feeling healthy, energetic, and optimistic, as all challenges are passing you by.

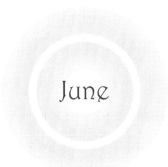

June

The next few weeks you will receive a sign, that certain projects requiring enormous efforts are coming to an end. But you will not give up without a fight, and this move is the right one!

Work. Mars is in your sign, which predicts a serious fight. Entrepreneurs are, once again, dealing with partners' hardline views when it comes to business. Once again, this is over differing views of how you envision the business developing, and in the most serious cases, you will go your separate ways.

Serious conflicts are likely with your adversaries during the middle and end of the month, but there will be no winners, yet. The feuding parties are refusing to budge. Your position is weak though, right now, so take advantage of anything you can, in order to protect yourself.

Employees are likely to experience yet another disagreement with management, as well as hostile colleagues. You might be dismissed, but you are not likely to have much to complain about there; you will still have the last word.

Your friends or mentors might be a glimmer of hope during all these painful processes. But not even they are all-powerful, nor are they always consistent or even without their own interests.

Money. Your financial situation is looking neutral. No major losses are expected for June, but your income is modest. The stars recommend that you try to save everywhere, as summer might be expensive, and future prospects are especially vague.

Love and family. Your family and personal life is rife with problems, in the case of many Leos.

Your spouse or partner might be going through hard times, and really need your support, right now. Their reaction, however, to your initiatives, might not be what you had planned or deserve.

Alternatively, serious arguments are a real possibility, due to both sides' hardline positions.

Friends' influence will somewhat improve things, but is unlikely to entirely resolve the problem.

If the roots of this confrontation are something that took place long ago, then either now, or next month, you will be able to put an end to relationships that ran their course long ago.

Health. You are feeling energetic in June, and are not expected to fall ill. You might start to feel slightly more tired during the last few days of the month, but if you live a healthy lifestyle and remember to get enough sleep, you should be able to avoid any trouble.

July

The best spot under the sun is never free. You need to examine this truth now.

Work. This month, the stars are urging you to pay attention to your relationship with business partners. Once again, conflict is brewing in this area of your life, and, most likely, it will come to light during the first ten days of July.

In some cases, this will involve the division of joint business, or some sort of compensation.

The stars recommend you haggle to the very end, and only then accepting conditions as they stand. But you are not likely to do that, so you may find yourself in a quagmire.

Alternatively, you may be seeking money to keep your business going. The astrologist does not envision this being particularly promising, but if you feel certain, then take this opportunity.

Employees might run into conflict with management, and think about another place for their talents. If that sounds like you, keep in mind that it may take a few months to find the right place, so remember to measure twice and cut once.

Money. Financially speaking, this month is rather challenging, though you will certainly not find yourself penniless. You will not see money coming in constantly, and are more likely to receive credit, sponsorship, or help from loved ones.

You may also get your share, if you are dividing up a business.

Love and family. During the first ten days of the month, your personal life looks tense and full of conflict. Of course, this involves couples who were already experiencing problems. Once again, you are thinking about divorce, but if you do not plan on ending the relationship, think about what you say, and avoid doing anything rash. If things have already been resolved, then this advice is superfluous.

Stable couples will overcome problems together, and that may include receiving help from a loved one, who supports you during difficult periods at work.

From July 11 to 31, many Leos might go on a vacation, deal with household matters, repairs, or interior renovations.

Stable families will also think about expanding their family, which will happen in the near future.

Health. This month, you are not particularly energetic, and that is most noticeable during the period of the New Moon, from July 9-11. Take care of yourself and remember that your health is the most important thing, and everything else will follow.

August

You celebrate your birth month ready for a fight. And you'll get a lot of what you hoped for!

Work. The astrologist suggests that Leos might be able to get the most out of a tricky situation causing you trouble during the first ten days of the month. Once again, the problem is serious disagreements with partners over your joint business. If you face heated debates during this period, during the second half of the month, the thorny issues may be at least partially resolved. In some cases, the root problem will be financial compensation for dividing up your business, and in others, both parties will find an acceptable compromise.

Employees can count on a decent payout should they be dismissed, but many of them will negotiate something with management from their old jobs. In any case, you will be pleased with the end results, so feel free to pursue your desires.

Money. Finances are not looking bad this month, and you might even say that August is one of the best times of the year for you. You can expect to receive the largest sums on August 1, 9, 19, 20, and 27-29.

Love and family. Many Leos will see major events underway at work, and leave their personal life on the back burner. However, those who fate has connected to their spouse through shared work, might experience conflict over your business's future, or dividing it up.

You are only likely to reach a compromise during the last ten days of the month, when many relationships will be at their most effective and productive. When it comes to any difficult, controversial issue, you can count on support from your relatives, who might serve as intermediaries between divorcing or fighting couples.

Health. This month, you are significantly more energetic, and you are quickly getting better after any illnesses last month.

September

You will feel confident in your efforts all month, and you have plenty of reasons for that!

Work. Professionally speaking, this month is one of your best in 2021. No matter what you are dealing with, you will see quick success.

Entrepreneurs are starting new business, and will also see profits from a previous project.

Employees might count on a raise this month, and in the best-case scenario, a job with a new, promising organization.

Old arguments with associates, legal problems, and other troubles are a thing of the past, and now, you have time to work on building a new future.

You are slowly reconnecting with previous associates, and most likely, they are colleagues from another city or abroad. During the first ten days of the month, you might begin negotiations, which will lead to positive results in the near future.

Try to finish all your important tasks and meetings by September 26 or 27, as Mercury will be in retrograde after that, and, most of the time, that means that everything will suddenly slow down.

Money. September might be one of the best months of 2021 when it comes to your finances. Money is coming in regularly, and there is significantly more of it. You can expect to receive the largest amounts on September 5-7, 14-16, and 24-26. Your expenses are low, predictable, and reasonable.

Love and family. Your personal life is currently on the back burner – work and money come first! But those who spend their days at home can count on a much better relationship with your loved ones.

If your marriage has been on the rocks, you might find that dedicated relatives are able to persuade you to reconcile. September may have fateful significance for couples; conflicts with parents are now a thing of the past, and you might make a decision about marriage or living arrangements.

Health. This September you are feeling healthy, energetic, confident, and that is a good sign that you have no reason to fear any illnesses. It is worth mentioning that the first twenty days of the month are a great time for shopping, changing your look, and other cosmetic procedures.

October

This month, you are jumping through some final hoops, which will have a positive effect on your work. Remember to follow your plan, and don't let the details pass you by.

Work. Entrepreneurs and managers will hold negotiations with partners in October, with varying success. Some will be slower than you had anticipated.

Work-related and administrative issues may become a stumbling block, and you will have to discuss them and deal with red tape. You might hold long consultations with attorneys, who will painstakingly pore over any legally required documents. This time, everything will take place peacefully, as both parties are tired of fighting.

The stars recommend being cautious and careful when looking over any documents required for work, as Mercury will be in retrograde from October 1 to 18. That means that any mistakes in important paperwork are highly likely. You are also likely to come across incorrect or deliberately twisted information.

This advice is also relevant for anyone planning on cooperating with colleagues from other cities or abroad. All month, remember the phrase, "trust but verify!"

Money. Your financial situation is looking uncertain this month. You might see money held up until the end of the month, when things will finally change. But that only applies to what you expect to come in, and you might also see money on October 3, 4, and 31.

Love and family. You are spending a lot of time with your relatives this month. These family ties might help you through a disagreement with your partner. If your loved one is having problems, then you can count on support from your own family.

If you have recently had a major argument or divorced, your relatives might help you deal with major issues involving property, and in case you and your partner are able to find common ground, assist with your reconciliation.

In the worst-case scenario, you will have to turn to a qualified attorney for help.

With help from relatives, couples will be able to overcome resistance from their parents, and you can expect to get married or move in together, soon.

Health. You are feeling healthy in October, especially if you are experiencing less stress, gossip, and getting to bed on time.

November

This month, it is worth temporarily putting your ambitions on hold. They aren't happening, right now. And that goes for both work and your personal life.

Work. You are facing one of the more difficult months of your work and career. Entrepreneurs and managers will once again find themselves facing conflict with associates when it comes to shared business. Any previous agreements will go out the window for the time being, and you are not the one expected to benefit from that.

If you recently did not get what you wanted, the stars warn that November is not the time to start trying to revise any agreements, even if you think that you have been slighted. November will bring nothing but conflict and emotional outbursts.

That advice is relevant for employees, too, as they are also going through a difficult time at work. You may see major changes underway at your organization, which will force you to think about leaving. It is not worth making any requests to management right now, or getting into any arguments with colleagues. Your best strategy is to take some time away and work on your home and family life, for now.

Money. November is not a promising month for your bank account, which is not surprising given the trends at work. Your expenses are not excessive, but you will not have any income, either. Keep an eye on your wallet and close to the end of November, you can expect a small amount of money to come in.

Love and family. Many Leos might be fully immersed in their personal life this month. You can expect problems in this area of your life, too, and they will beset both stable couples, and those whose relationships have been on the rocks for some time.

There is a strong possibility that your lives are about to go in different directions, and you will prefer it this way. This is the path the planets will take you on during the first twenty days of November.

Closer to the end of the month, however, children may serve as a bridge between warring spouses, and you should take advantage of this if you are wavering in your decision. If you have no doubts, then that advice is superfluous.

Alternatively, your loved one will face problems, which will worry the entire family. If this describes you, be patient, and help everyone, however you can.

Health. This month, you are feeling less than energetic, so take care of yourself and be vigilant.

December

The end of the year will be a busy time, and you are sure to see a variety of events taking place. There is nothing you can do about that, it's just life!

Work. Your biggest problem in December will be your relationship with a business partner. You will have constant disagreements related to different visions of your business, and you may even part ways. This is most likely at the beginning and end of December.

This is an issue that has been going on for a while, and either improved or worsened, but now it is D-Day, and you will have to resolve this stagnant conflict, one way or another. What do you do? Only you can decide. You may decide to take out credit and buy out your adversaries in order to take the business yourself. Alternatively, you might receive a payment for your share, while your former business partner takes the rest.

You are unlikely to be capable of working together anymore, so each party might choose the option that is most favorable to themselves.

Things look much easier for employees – they can turn to management and strengthen their own fragile position.

Money. Your finances are looking unstable in December. You will have income, but you have massive expenses, and most of it is related to your home, family, children, or romantic relationships.

Love and family. Your family life is looking rather calm. Couples in a stable marriage will be busy with repairs, and they may decide to re-do their interiors. Many will resolve problems related to their children, and invest in their training, education, and development, which will take up a large chunk of the family budget.

Divorced and divorcing couples might have difficulty resolving residual issues involving property, and there is hope that this month, their saga will finally come to an end.

For many Leos, December is a time of celebrations, birthdays, and reconnecting with old friends and lovers. You might rekindle an old romance, and wonder about its future. You will spend the holidays themselves with children and your closest loved ones, however.

Health. This month, you will be healthy, energetic, and spared by any illness.

A guide to Zodiac compatibility

Often, when we meet a person, we get a feeling that they are good and we take an instant liking to them. Another person, however, gives us immediate feelings of distrust, fear and hostility. Is there an astrological reason why people say that 'the first impression is the most accurate'? How can we detect those who will bring us nothing but trouble and unhappiness?

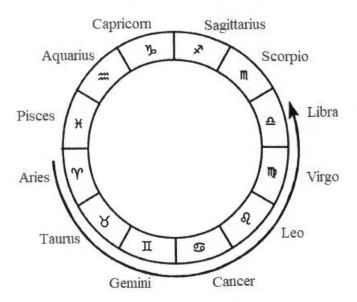

Without going too deeply into astrological subtleties unfamiliar to some readers, it is possible to determine the traits according to which friendship, love or business relationships will develop.

Let's begin with problematic relationships - our most difficult are with our **8th sign**. For example, for Aries the 8th sign is Scorpio, for Taurus it is Sagittarius and so on. Finding your 8th sign is easy; assume your own sign to be first (see above Figure) and then move eight signs counter clockwise around the Zodiac circle. This is also how the other signs (fourth, ninth and so on) that we mention are to be found.

Ancient astrologers variously referred to the 8th sign as the symbol of death, of destruction, of fated love or unfathomable attraction. In astrological terms, this pair is called 'master and slave' or 'boa constrictor and rabbit', with the role of 'master' or 'boa constrictor' being played by our 8th sign.

This relationship is especially difficult for politicians and business people.

We can take the example of a recent political confrontation in the USA. Hilary Clinton is a Scorpio while Donald Trump is a Gemini - her 8th sign. Even though many were certain that Clinton would be elected President, she lost.

To take another example, Hitler was a Taurus and his opponents – Stalin and Churchill - were both of his 8th sign, Sagittarius. The result of their confrontation is well known. Interestingly, the Russian Marshals who dealt crushing military blows to Hitler and so helped end the Third Reich - Konstantin Rokossovsky and Georgy Zhukov - were also Sagittarian, Hitler's 8th sign.

In another historical illustration, Lenin was also a Taurus. Stalin was of Lenin's 8th sign and was ultimately responsible for the downfall and possibly death of his one-time comrade-in-arms.

Business ties with those of our 8th sign are hazardous as they ultimately lead to stress and loss; both financial and moral. So, do not tangle with your 8th sign and never fight with it - your chances of winning are remote!

Such relationships are very interesting in terms of love and romance, however. We are magnetically attracted to our 8th sign and even though it may be very intense physically, it is very difficult for family life;

'Feeling bad when together, feeling worse when apart'.

As an example, let us take the famous lovers - George Sand who was Cancer and Alfred de Musset who was Sagittarius. Cancer is the 8th sign for Sagittarius, and the story of their crazy two-year love affair was the subject of much attention throughout France. Critics and writers were divided into 'Mussulist' and 'Sandist' camps; they debated fiercely about who was to blame for the sad ending to their love story - him or her. It's hard to imagine the energy needed to captivate the public for so long, but that energy was destructive for the couple. Passion raged in their hearts, but neither of them was able to comprehend their situation.

Georges Sand wrote to Musset, "*I•on't love you anymore, an• I will always a•ore you. I •on't want you anymore, an• I can't •o without you. It seems that nothing but a heavenly lightning strike can heal me by •estroying me. Goo•-bye! Stay or go, but •on't say that I am not suffering. This is the only thing that can make me suffer even more, my love, my life, my bloo•! Go away, but kill me, leaving.*" Musset replied only in brief, but its power surpassed Sand's tirade, "*When you embrace• me, I felt something that is still bothering me, making it impossible for me to approach another woman.*" These two people loved each other passionately and for two years lived together in a powder keg of passion, hatred and treachery.

When someone enters into a romantic liaison with their 8th sign, there will be no peace; indeed, these relationships are very attractive to those who enjoy the edgy, the borderline and, in the Dostoevsky style, the melodramatic. The first to lose interest in the relationship is, as a rule, the 8th sign.

If, by turn of fate, our child is born under our 8th sign, they will be very different from us and, in some ways, not live up to our expectations. It may be best to let them choose their own path.

In business and political relationships, the combination with our **12th sign** is also a complicated one.

We can take two political examples. Angela Merkel is a Cancer while Donald Trump is a Gemini - her 12th sign. This is why their relations are strained and complicated and we can even perhaps assume that the American president will achieve his political goals at her expense. Boris Yeltsin (Aquarius) was the 12th sign to Mikhail Gorbachev (Pisces) and it was Yeltsin who managed to dethrone the champion of Perestroika.

Even ancient astrologers noticed that our relationships with our 12th signs can never develop evenly; it is one of the most curious and problematic combinations. They are our hidden enemies and they seem to be digging a hole for us; they ingratiate themselves with us, discover our innermost secrets. As a result, we become bewildered and make mistakes when we deal with them. Among the Roman emperors murdered by members of their entourage, there was an interesting pattern - all the murderers were the 12th sign of the murdered.

We can also see this pernicious effect in Russian history: the German princess Alexandra (Gemini) married the last Russian Tsar Nicholas II (Taurus) - he was her 12th sign and brought her a tragic death. The wicked genius Grigory Rasputin (Cancer) made friends with Tsarina Alexandra, who was his 12th sign, and was murdered as a result of their odd friendship. The weakness of Nicholas II was exposed, and his authority reduced after the death of the economic and social reformer Pyotr Stolypin, who was his 12th sign. Thus, we see a chain of people whose downfall was brought about by their 12th sign.

So, it makes sense to be cautious of your 12th sign, especially if you have business ties. Usually, these people know much more about us than we want them to and they will often reveal our secrets for personal gain if it suits them. However, the outset of these relationships is, as a rule, quite normal - sometimes the two people will be friends, but sooner or later one will betray the other one or divulge a secret; inadvertently or not.

In terms of romantic relationships, our 12th sign is gentle, they take care of us and are tender towards us. They know our weaknesses well but accept them with understanding. It is they who guide us, although sometimes almost imperceptibly. Sexual attraction is usually strong.

For example, Meghan Markle is a Leo, the 12th sign for Prince Harry, who is a Virgo. Despite Queen Elizabeth II being lukewarm about the match, Harry's love was so strong that they did marry.

If a child is our 12th sign, it later becomes clear that they know all our secrets, even those that they are not supposed to know. It is very difficult to control them as they do everything in their own way.

Relations with our 7th **sign** are also interesting. They are like our opposite; they have something to learn from us while we, in turn, have something to learn from them. This combination, in business and personal relationships, can be very positive and stimulating provided that both partners are quite intelligent and have high moral standards but if not, constant misunderstandings and challenges follow. Marriage or co-operation with the 7th sign can only exist as the union of two fully-fledged individuals and in this case love, significant business achievements and social success are possible.

However, the combination can be not only interesting, but also quite complicated.

An example is Angelina Jolie, a Gemini, and Brad Pitt, a Sagittarius. This is a typical bond with a 7th sign - it's lively and interesting, but rather stressful. Although such a couple may quarrel and even part from time to time, never do they lose interest in each other.

This may be why this combination is more stable in middle-age when there is an understanding of the true nature of marriage and partnership. In global, political terms, this suggests a state of eternal tension - a cold war - for example between Yeltsin (Aquarius) and Bill Clinton (Leo).

Relations with our 9th **sign** are very good; they are our teacher and advisor - one who reveals things we are unaware of and our relationships with them very often involve travel or re-location. The combination can lead to spiritual growth and can be beneficial in terms of business.

Although, for example, Trump and Putin are political opponents, they can come to an understanding and even feel a certain sympathy for each other because Putin is a Libra while Trump is a Gemini, his 9th sign.

This union is also quite harmonious for conjugal and romantic relationships.

We treat our **3rd sign** somewhat condescendingly. They are like our younger siblings; we teach them and expect them to listen attentively. Our younger brothers and sisters are more often than not born under this sign. In terms of personal and sexual relationships, the union is not very inspiring and can end quickly, although this is not always the case. In terms of business, it is fairly average as it often connects partners from different cities or countries.

We treat our **5th sign** as a child and we must take care of them accordingly. The combination is not very good for business, however, since our 5th sign triumphs over us in terms of connections and finances, and thereby gives us very little in return save for love or sympathy. However, they are very good for family and romantic relationships, especially if the 5th sign is female. If a child is born as a 5th sign to their parents, their relationship will be a mutually smooth, loving and understanding one that lasts a lifetime.

Our **10th sign** is a born leader. Depending on the spiritual level of those involved, both pleasant and tense relations are possible; the relationship is often mutually beneficial in the good times but mutually disruptive in the bad times. In family relations, our 10th sign always tries to lead and will do so according to their intelligence and upbringing.

Our **4th sign** protects our home and can act as a sponsor to strengthen our financial or moral positions. Their advice should be heeded in all cases as it can be very effective, albeit very unobtrusive. If a woman takes this role, the relationship can be long and romantic, since all the spouse's wishes are usually met one way or another. Sometimes, such couples achieve great social success; for instance, Hilary Clinton, a Scorpio is the 4th sign to Bill Clinton, a Leo. On the other hand, if the husband is the 4th sign for his wife, he tends to be henpecked. There is often a strong sexual attraction. Our 4th sign can improve our living conditions and care for us in a parental way. If a child is our 4th sign, they are close to us and support us affectionately.

Relations with our **11th sign** are often either friendly or patronizing; we treat them reverently, while they treat us with friendly condescension. Sometimes, these relationships develop in an 'older brother' or 'high-ranking friend' sense; indeed, older brothers and sisters are often our 11th sign. In terms of personal and sexual relationships, our 11th sign is always inclined to enslave us. This tendency is most clearly manifested in such alliances as Capricorn and Pisces or Leo and Libra. A child who is the 11th sign to their parents will achieve greater success than their parents, but this will only make the parents proud.

Our **2nd sign** should bring us financial or other benefits; we receive a lot from them in both our business and our family life. In married couples, the 2nd sign usually looks after the financial situation for the benefit of the family. Sexual attraction is strong.

Our **6th sign** is our 'slave'; we always benefit from working with them and it's very difficult for them to escape our influence. In the event of hostility, especially if they have provoked the conflict, they receive a powerful retaliatory strike. In personal relations, we can almost destroy them by making them dance to our tune. For example, if a husband doesn't allow his wife to work or there are other adverse family circumstances, she gradually becomes lost as an individual despite being surrounded by care. This is the best-case scenario; worse outcomes are possible. Our 6th sign has a strong sexual attraction to us because we are the fatal 8th sign for them; we cool down quickly, however, and often make all kinds of demands. If the relationship with our 6th sign is a long one, there is a danger that routine, boredom and stagnation will ultimately destroy the relationship. A child born under our 6th sign needs particularly careful handling as they can feel fear or embarrassment when communicating with us. Their health often needs increased attention and we should also remember that they are very different from us emotionally.

Finally, we turn to relations with **our own sign**. Scorpio with Scorpio and Cancer with Cancer get along well, but in most other cases, however, our own sign is of little interest to us as it has a similar energy. Sometimes, this relationship can develop as a rivalry, either in business or in love.

There is another interesting detail - we are often attracted to one particular sign. For example, a man's wife and mistress often have the same sign. If there is confrontation between the two, the stronger character displaces the weaker one. As an example, Prince Charles is a Scorpio, while both Princess Diana and Camilla Parker Bowles were born under the sign of Cancer. Camilla was the more assertive and became dominant.

Of course, in order to draw any definitive conclusions, we need an individually prepared horoscope, but the above always, one way or another, manifests itself.

Love description of Zodiac Signs

We know that human sexual behavior has been studied at length. Entire libraries have been written about it, with the aim of helping us understand ourselves and our partners. But is that even possible? It may not be; no matter how smart we are, when it comes to love and sex, there is always an infinite amount to learn. But we have to strive for perfection, and astrology, with its millennia of research, twelve astrological types, and twelve zodiac signs, may hold the key. Below, you will find a brief and accurate description of each zodiac sign's characteristics in love, for both men and women.

Men

ARIES

Aries men are not particularly deep or wise, but they make up for it in sincerity and loyalty. They are active, even aggressive lovers, but a hopeless romantic may be lurking just below the surface. Aries are often monogamous and chivalrous men, for whom there is only one woman (of course, in her absence, they can sleep around with no remorse). If the object of your affection is an Aries, be sure to give him a lot of sex, and remember that for an Aries, when it comes to sex, anything goes. Aries cannot stand women who are negative or disheveled. They need someone energetic, lively, and to feel exciting feelings of romance.

The best partner for an Aries is Cancer, Sagittarius, or Leo. Aquarius can also be a good match, but the relationship will be rather friendly in nature. Partnering with a Scorpio or Taurus will be difficult, but they can be stimulating lovers for an Aries. Virgos are good business contacts, but a poor match as lovers or spouses.

TAURUS

A typical Taurean man is warm, friendly, gentle, and passionate, even if he doesn't always show it. He is utterly captivated by the beauty of the female body, and can find inspiration in any woman. A Taurus has such excess physical and sexual prowess, that to him, sex is a way to relax and calm down. He is the most passionate and emotional lover of the Zodiac, but he expects his partner to take the initiative, and if she doesn't, he will easily find someone else. Taureans rarely divorce, and are true to the end – if not sexually, at least spiritually. They are secretive, keep their cards close, and may have secret lovers. If a Taurus does not feel a deep emotional connection with someone, he won't be shy to ask her friends for their number. He prefers a voluptuous figure over an athletic or skinny woman.

The best partners for a Taurus are Cancer, Virgo, Pisces, or Scorpio. Sagittarius can show a Taurus real delights in both body and spirit, but they are unlikely to make it down the aisle. They can have an interesting relationship with an Aquarius – these signs are very different, but sometimes can spend their lives together. They might initially feel attracted to an Aries, before rejecting her.

GEMINI

The typical Gemini man is easygoing and polite. He is calm, collected, and analytical. For a Gemini, passion is closely linked to intellect, to the point that they will try to find an explanation for their actions before carrying them out. But passion cannot be explained, which scares a Gemini, and they begin jumping from one extreme to the other. This is why you will find more bigamists among Geminis than any other sign of the Zodiac. Sometimes, Gemini men even have two families, or divorce and marry several times throughout the course of their lives. This may be because they simply can't let new and interesting experiences pass them by. A Gemini's wife or lover needs to be smart, quick, and always looking ahead. If she isn't, he will find a new object for his affection.

Aquarians, Libras, and Aries make good partners for a Gemini. A Sagittarius can be fascinating for him, but they will not marry before he reaches middle age, as both partners will be fickle while they are younger. A Gemini and Scorpio are likely to be a difficult match, and the Gemini will try to wriggle out of the Scorpio's tight embrace. A Taurus will be an exciting sex partner, but their partnership won't be for long, and the Taurus is often at fault.

CANCER

Cancers tend to be deep, emotional individuals, who are both sensitive and highly sexual. Their charm is almost mystical, and they know how to use it. Cancers may be the most promiscuous sign of the Zodiac, and open to absolutely anything in bed. Younger Cancers look for women who are more mature, as they are skilled lovers. As they age, they look for someone young enough to be their own daughter, and delight in taking on the role of a teacher. Cancers are devoted to building a family and an inviting home, but once they achieve that goal, they are likely to have a wandering eye. They will not seek moral justification, as they sincerely believe it is simply something everyone does. Their charm works in such a way that women are deeply convinced they are the most important love in a Cancer's life, and that circumstances are the only thing preventing them from being together. Remember that a Cancer man is a master manipulator, and will not be yours unless he is sure you have throngs of admirers. He loves feminine curves, and is turned on by exquisite fragrances. Cancers don't end things with old lovers, and often go back for a visit after a breakup. Another type of Cancer is rarer – a faithful friend, and up for anything in order to provide for his wife and children. He is patriotic and a responsible worker.

Scorpios, Pisces, and other Cancers are a good match. A Taurus can make for a lasting relationship, as both signs place great value on family and are able to get along with one another. A Sagittarius will result in fights and blowouts from the very beginning, followed by conflicts and breakups. The Sagittarius will suffer the most. Marriage to an Aries isn't off the table, but it won't last very long.

LEO

A typical Leo is handsome, proud, and vain, with a need to be the center of attention at all times. They often pretend to be virtuous, until they are able to actually master it. They crave flattery, and prefer women who comply and cater to them. Leos demand unconditional obedience, and constant approval. When a Leo is in love, he is fairly sexual, and capable of being devoted and faithful. Cheap love affairs are not his thing, and Leos are highly aware of how expensive it is to divorce. They make excellent fathers. A Leo's partner needs to look polished and well-dressed, and he will not tolerate either frumpiness or nerds.

Aries, Sagittarius, and Gemini make for good matches. Leos are often very beguiling to Libras; this is the most infamous astrological "master-slave" pairing. Leos are also inexplicably drawn to Pisces – this is the only sign capable of taming them. A Leo and Virgo will face a host of problems sooner or later, and they might be material in nature. The Virgo will attempt to conquer him, and if she does, a breakup is inevitable.

VIRGO

Virgo is a highly intellectual sign, who likes to take a step back and spend his time studying the big picture. But love inherently does not lend itself to analysis, and this can leave Virgos feeling perplexed. While Virgo is taking his time, studying the object of his affection, someone else will swoop in and take her away, leaving him bitterly disappointed. Perhaps for that reason, Virgos tend to marry late, but once they are married, they remain true, and hardly ever initiate divorce. In bed, they are modest and reserved, as they see sex as some sort of quirk of nature, designed solely for procreation. Most Virgos have a gifted sense of taste, hearing, and smell. They cannot tolerate pungent odors and can be squeamish; they believe their partners should always take pains to be very clean. Virgos usually hate over-the-top expressions of love, and are immune to sex as a mean s of control. Many Virgos are stingy and more appropriate as husbands than lovers. Male Virgos tend to be monogamous, though if they are unhappy or disappointed with their partner, they may begin to look for comfort elsewhere and often give in to drunkenness.

Taurus, Capricorn, and Scorpio make the best partners for a Virgo. They may feel inexplicable attraction for Aquarians. They will form friendships with Aries, but rarely will this couple make it down the aisle. With Leos, be careful – this sign is best as a lover, not a spouse.

LIBRA

Libra is a very complex, wishy-washy sign. They are constantly seeking perfection, which often leaves them in discord with the reality around them. Libra men are elegant and refined, and expect no less from their partner. Many Libras treat their partners like a beautiful work of art, and have trouble holding onto the object of their affection. They view love itself as a very abstract concept, and can get tired of the physical aspect of their relationship. They are much more drawn to intrigue and the chase- dreams, candlelit evenings, and other symbols of romance. A high percentage of Libra men are gay, and they view sex with other men as the more elite option. Even when Libras are unhappy in their marriages, they never divorce willingly. Their wives might leave them, however, or they might be taken away by a more decisive partner.

Aquarius and Gemini make the best matches for Libras. Libra can also easily control an independent Sagittarius, and can easily fall under the influence of a powerful and determined Leo, before putting all his strength and effort into breaking free. Relationships with Scorpios are difficult; they may become lovers, but will rarely marry.

SCORPIO

Though it is common to perceive Scorpios as incredibly sexual, they are, in fact, very unassuming, and never brag about their exploits. They will, however, be faithful and devoted to the right woman. The Scorpio man is taciturn, and you can't expect any tender words from him, but he will defend those he loves to the very end. Despite his outward control, Scorpio is very emotional; he needs and craves love, and is willing to fight for it. Scorpios are incredible lovers, and rather than leaving them tired, sex leaves them feeling energized. They are always sexy, even if they aren't particularly handsome. They are unconcerned with the ceremony of wooing you, and more focused on the act of love itself.

Expressive Cancers and gentle, amenable Pisces make the best partners. A Scorpio might also fall under the spell of a Virgo, who is adept at taking the lead. Sparks might fly between two Scorpios, or with a Taurus, who is perfect for a Scorpio in bed. Relationships with Libras, Sagittarians, and Aries are difficult.

SAGITTARIUS

Sagittarian men are lucky, curious, and gregarious. Younger Sagittarians are romantic, passionate, and burning with desire to experience every type of love. Sagittarius is a very idealistic sign, and in that search for perfection, they tend to flit from one partner to another, eventually forgetting what they were even looking for in the first place. A negative Sagittarius might have two or three relationships going on at once, assigning each partner a different day of the week. On the other hand, a positive Sagittarius will channel his powerful sexual energy into creativity, and take his career to new heights. Generally speaking, after multiple relationships and divorces, the Sagittarian man will conclude that his ideal marriage is one where his partner is willing to look the other way.

Aries and Leo make the best matches for a Sagittarius. He might fall under the spell of a Cancer, but would not be happy being married to her. Gemini can be very intriguing, but will only make for a happy marriage after middle age, when both partners are older and wiser. Younger Sagittarians often marry Aquarian women, but things quickly fall apart. Scorpios can make for an interesting relationship, but if the Sagittarius fails to comply, divorce is inevitable.

CAPRICORN

Practical, reserved Capricorn is one of the least sexual signs of the Zodiac. He views sex as an idle way to pass the time, and something he can live without, until he wants to start a family. He tends to marry late, and almost never divorces. Young Capricorns are prone to suppressing their sexual desires, and only discover them later in life, when they have already achieved everything a real man needs – a career and money. We'll be frank – Capricorn is not the best lover, but he can compensate by being caring, attentive, and showering you with valuable gifts. Ever cautious, Capricorn loves to schedule his sexual relationships, and this is something partners will just have to accept. Women should understand that Capricorn needs some help relaxing – perhaps with alcohol. They prefer inconspicuous, unassuming women, and run away from a fashion plate.

The best partners for a Capricorn are Virgo, Taurus, or Scorpio. Cancers might catch his attention, and if they marry, it is likely to be for life. Capricorn is able to easily dominate Pisces, and Pisces-Capricorn is a well-known "slave and master" combination. Relationships with Leos tend to be erratic, and they are unlikely to wed. Aries might make for a cozy family at first, but things will cool off quickly, and often, the marriage only lasts as long as Capricorn is unwilling to make a change in his life.

AQUARIUS

Aquarian men are mercurial, and often come off as peculiar, unusual, or aloof, and detached. Aquarians are turned on by anything novel or strange, and they are constantly looking for new and interesting people. They are stimulated by having a variety of sexual partners, but they consider this to simply be normal life, rather than sexually immoral. Aquarians are unique – they are more abstract than realistic, and can be cold and incomprehensible, even in close relationships. Once an Aquarius gets married, he will try to remain within the realm of decency, but often fails. An Aquarian's partners need uncommon patience, as nothing they do can restrain him. Occasionally, one might encounter another kind of Aquarius – a responsible, hard worker, and exemplary family man.

The best matches for an Aquarius are female fellow Aquarians, Libras, and Sagittarians. When Aquarius seeks out yet another affair, he is not choosy, and will be happy with anyone.

PISCES

Pisces is the most eccentric sign of the Zodiac. This is reflected in his romantic tendencies and sex life. Pisces men become very dependent on those with whom they have a close relationship. Paradoxically, they are simultaneously crafty and childlike when it comes to playing games, and they are easily deceived. As a double bodied sign, Pisces rarely marry just once, as they are very sexual, easily fall in love, and are constantly seeking their ideal. Pisces are very warm people, who love to take care of others and are inclined toward "slave-master" relationships, in which they are the submissive partner. But after catering to so many lovers, Pisces will remain elusive. They are impossible to figure out ahead of time – today, they might be declaring their love for you, but tomorrow, they may disappear – possibly forever! To a Pisces, love is a fantasy, illusion, and dream, and they might spend their whole lives in pursuit of it. Pisces who are unhappy in love are vulnerable to alcoholism or drug addiction.

Cancer and Scorpio make the best partners for a Pisces. He is also easily dominated by Capricorn and Libra, but in turn will conquer even a queen-like Leo. Often, they are fascinated by Geminis – if they marry, it will last a long time, but likely not forever. Relationships with Aries and Sagittarians are erratic, though initially, things can seem almost perfect.

Women

ARIES

Aries women are leaders. They are decisive, bold, and very protective. An Aries can take initiative and is not afraid to make the first move. Her ideal man is strong, and someone she can admire. But remember, at the slightest whiff of weakness, she will knock him off his pedestal. She does not like dull, whiny men, and thinks that there is always a way out of any situation. If she loves someone, she will be faithful. Aries women are too honest to try leading a double life. They are possessive, jealous, and not only will they not forgive those who are unfaithful, their revenge may be brutal; they know no limits. If you can handle an Aries, don't try to put her in a cage; it is best to give her a long leash. Periodically give her some space – then she will seek you out herself. She is sexual, and believe that anything goes in bed.

Her best partners are a Sagittarius or Leo. A Libra can make a good match after middle age, once both partners have grown wiser and settled down a bit. Gemini and Aquarius are only good partners during the initial phase, when everything is still new, but soon enough, they will lose interest in each other. Scorpios are good matches in bed, but only suitable as lovers.

TAURUS

Taurean women possess qualities that men often dream about, but rarely find in the flesh – they are soft, charming, practical, and reliable – they are very caring and will support their partner in every way. A Taurus is highly sexual, affectionate, and can show a man how to take pleasure to new heights. She is also strong and intense. If she is in love, she will be faithful. But when love fades away, she might find someone else on the side, though she will still fight to save her marriage, particularly if her husband earns good money. A Taurus will not tolerate a man who is disheveled or disorganized, and anyone dating her needs to always be on his toes. She will expect gifts, and likes being taken to expensive restaurants, concerts, and other events. If you argue, try to make the first peace offering, because a Taurus finds it very hard to do so – she might withdraw and ruminate for a long time. Never air your dirty laundry; solve all your problems one-on-one.

Scorpio, Virgo, Capricorn, and Cancer make the best matches. A relationship with an Aries or Sagittarius would be difficult. There is little attraction between a Taurus and a Leo, and initially Libras can make for a good partner in bed, but things will quickly cool off and fall apart. A Taurus and Aquarius make an interesting match – despite the difference in signs, their relationships are often lasting, and almost lifelong.

GEMINI

Gemini women are social butterflies, outgoing, and they easily make friends, and then break off the friendship, if people do not hold their interest. A Gemini falls in love hard, is very creative, and often fantasizes about the object of her affection. She is uninterested in sex without any attachment, loves to flirt, and, for the most part, is not particularly affectionate. She dreams of a partner who is her friend, lover, and a romantic, all at once. A Gemini has no use for a man who brings nothing to the table intellectually. That is a tall order, so Geminis often divorce and marry several times. Others simply marry later in life. Once you have begun a life together, do not try to keep her inside – she needs to travel, explore, socialize, attend events and go to the theater. She cannot tolerate possessive men, so avoid giving her the third degree, and remember that despite her flirtatious and social nature, she is, in fact, faithful – as long as you keep her interested and she is in love. Astrologists believe that Geminis do not know what they need until age 29 or 30, so it is best to hold off on marriage until then.

Leo and Libra make the best matches. A relationship with a Cancer is likely, though complex, and depends solely on the Cancer's affection. A Gemini and Sagittarius can have an interesting, dynamic relationship, but these are two restless signs, which might only manage to get together after ages 40-45, once they have had enough thrills out of life and learned to be patient. Relationships with a Capricorn are very difficult, and almost never happen. The honeymoon stage can be wonderful with a Scorpio, but each partner will eventually go their own way, before ending things. A Gemini and Pisces union can also be very interesting – they are drawn to each other, and can have a wonderful relationship, but after a while, the cracks start to show and things will fall apart. An Aquarius is also not a bad match, but they will have little sexual chemistry.

CANCER

Cancers can be divided into two opposing groups. The first includes a sweet and gentle creature who is willing to dedicate her life to her husband and children. She is endlessly devoted to her husband, especially if he makes a decent living and remains faithful. She views all men as potential husbands, which means it is dangerous to strike up a relationship with her if your intentions are not serious; she can be anxious and clingy, sensitive and prone to crying. It is better to break things to her gently, rather than directly spitting out the cold, hard truth. She wants a man who can be a provider, though she often earns well herself. She puts money away for a rainy day, and knows how to be thrifty, for the sake of others around her, rather than only for herself. She is an excellent cook and capable of building an inviting home for her loved ones. She is enthusiastic in bed, a wonderful wife, and a caring mother.

The second type of Cancer is neurotic, and capable of creating a living hell for those around her. She believes that the world is her enemy, and manages to constantly find new intrigue and machinations.

Another Cancer, Virgo, Taurus, Scorpio, and Pisces make the best matches. A Cancer can often fall in love with a Gemini, but eventually, things will grow complicated, as she will be exhausted by a Gemini's constant mood swings and cheating. A Cancer and Sagittarius will initially have passionate sex, but things will quickly cool off. A relationship with a Capricorn is a real possibility, but only later in life, as while they are young, they are likely to fight and argue constantly. Cancer can also have a relationship with an Aries, but this will not be easy.

LEO

Leos are usually beautiful or charming, and outwardly sexual. And yet, appearances can be deceiving – they are not actually that interested in sex. Leo women want to be the center of attention and men running after them boôsts their self-esteem, but they are more interested in their career, creating something new, and success than sex. They often have high-powered careers and are proud of their own achievements. Their partners need to be strong; if a Leo feels a man is weak, she can carry him herself for a while- before leaving him. It is difficult for her to find a partner for life, as chivalrous knights are a dying breed, and she is not willing to compromise. If you are interested in a Leo, take the initiative, admire her, and remember that even a queen is still a woman. Timid men or tightwads need not apply. Leos like to help others, but they don't need a walking disaster in their life. If they are married and in love, they are usually faithful, and petty gossip isn't their thing. Leo women make excellent mothers, and are ready to give their lives to their children. Their negative traits include vanity and a willingness to lie, in order to make themselves look better.

Sagittarius, Aries, and Libra make the best matches. Leos can also have an interesting relationship with a Virgo, though both partners will weaken each other. Life with a Taurus will lead to endless arguments – both signs are very stubborn, and unwilling to give in. Leos and Pisces are another difficult pair, as she will have to learn to be submissive if she wants to keep him around. A relationship with a Capricorn will work if there is a common denominator, but they will have little sexual chemistry. Life with a Scorpio will be turbulent to say the least, and they will usually break up later in life.

VIRGO

Virgo women are practical, clever, and often duplicitous. Marrying one isn't for everyone. She is a neat freak to the point of annoying those around her. She is also an excellent cook, and strives to ensure her children receive the very best by teaching them everything, and preparing them for a bright future. She is also thrifty – she won't throw money around, and, in fact, won't even give it to her husband. She has no time for rude, macho strongmen, and is suspicious of spendthrifts. She will not be offended if you take her to a cozy and modest café rather than an elegant restaurant. Virgos are masters of intrigue, and manage to outperform every other sign of the Zodiac in this regard. Virgos love to criticize everyone and everything; to listen to them, the entire world is simply a disaster and wrong, and only she is the exception to this rule. Virgos are not believed to be particularly sexual, but there are different variations when it comes to this. Rarely, one finds an open-minded Virgo willing to try anything, and who does it all on a grand scale – but she is rather the exception to this general rule.

The best matches for a Virgo are Cancer, Taurus, and Capricorn. She also can get along well with a Scorpio, but will find conflict with Sagittarius. A Pisces will strike her interest, but they will rarely make it down the aisle. She is often attracted to an Aquarius, but they would drive each other up the wall were they to actually marry. An Aries forces Virgo to see another side of life, but here, she will have to learn to conform and adapt.

LIBRA

Female Libras tend to be beautiful, glamorous, or very charming. They are practical, tactical, rational, though they are adept at hiding these qualities behind their romantic and elegant appearance. Libras are drawn to marriage, and are good at imagining the kind of partner they need. They seek out strong, well-off men and are often more interested in someone's social status and bank account than feelings. The object of their affection needs to be dashing, and have a good reputation in society. Libras love expensive things, jewelry, and finery. If they are feeling down, a beautiful gift will instantly cheer them up. They will not tolerate scandal or conflict, and will spend all their energy trying to keep the peace, or at least the appearance thereof. They do not like to air their dirty laundry, and will only divorce in extreme circumstances. They are always convinced they are right and react to any objections as though they have been insulted. Most Libras are not particularly sexual, except those with Venus or the Moon in Scorpio.

Leos, Geminis, and Aquarians make good matches. Libra women are highly attracted to Aries men - this is a real case of opposites attract. They can get along with a Sagittarius, though he will find that Libras are too proper and calm. Capricorn, Pisces, and Cancer are all difficult matches. Things will begin tumultuously with a Taurus, before each partner goes his or her own way.

SCORPIO

Scorpio women may appear outwardly restrained, but there is much more bubbling below the surface. They are ambitious with high self-esteem, but often wear a mask of unpretentiousness. They are the true power behind the scenes, the one who holds the family together, but never talk about it. Scorpios are strong-willed, resilient, and natural survivors. Often, Scorpios are brutally honest, and expect the same out of those around them. They do not like having to conform, and attempt to get others to adapt to them, as they honestly believe everyone will be better off that way. They are incredibly intuitive, and not easily deceived. They have an excellent memory, and can quickly figure out which of your buttons to push. They are passionate in bed, and their temperament will not diminish with age. When she is sexually frustrated, a Scorpio will throw all of her energy into her career or her loved ones. She is proud, categorical, and "if you don't do it right, don't do it at all" is her motto. Scorpio cannot be fooled, and she will not forgive any cheating. Will she cheat herself? Yes! But it will not break up her family, and she will attempt to keep it a secret. Scorpios are usually attractive to men, even if they are not particularly beautiful. They keep a low profile, though they always figure out their partner, and give them some invisible sign. There is also another, selfish type of Scorpio, who will use others for as long as they need them, before unceremoniously casting them aside.

Taurus is a good match; they will have excellent sexual chemistry and understand each other. Scorpio and Gemini are drawn to each other, but are unlikely to stay together long enough to actually get married. Cancer can be a good partner as well, but Cancers are possessive, while Scorpios do not like others meddling in their affairs, though they can later resolve their arguments in bed. Scorpio and Leo are often found together, but their relationship can also be very complicated. Leos are animated and chipper, while Scorpios, who are much deeper and more stubborn, see Leos as not particularly serious or reliable. One good example of this is Bill (a Leo) and Hillary (a Scorpio) Clinton. Virgo can also make a good partner, but when Scorpio seemingly lacks emotions, he will look for them elsewhere. Relationships with Lira are strange and very rare. Scorpio sees Libra as too insecure, and Libra does not appreciate Scorpio's rigidity. Two Scorpios together make an excellent marriage! Sagittarius and Scorpio are unlikely to get together, as she will think he is shallow and rude. If they do manage to get married, Scorpio's drive and persistence is the only thing that will make the marriage last. Capricorn is also not a bad match, and while Scorpio finds Aquarius attractive, they will rarely get married, as they are simply speaking different languages! Things are alright with a Pisces, as both signs are emotional, and Pisces can let Scorpio take the lead when necessary.

SAGITTARIUS

Sagittarius women are usually charming, bubbly, energetic, and have the gift of gab. They are kind, sincere, and love people. They are also straightforward, fair, and very ambitious, occasionally to the point of irritating those around them. But telling them something is easier than not telling them, and they often manage to win over their enemies. Sagittarius tends to have excellent intuition, and she loves to both learn and teach others. She is a natural leader, and loves taking charge at work and at home. Many Sagittarian women have itchy feet, and prefer all kinds of travel to sitting at home. They are not particularly good housewives – to be frank, cooking and cleaning is simply not for them. Their loved ones must learn to adapt to them, but Sagittarians themselves hate any pressure. They are not easy for men to handle, as Sagittarians want to be in charge. Sagittarius falls in love easily, is very sexual and temperamental, and may marry multiple times. Despite outward appearances, Sagittarius is a very lonely sign. Even after she is married with children, she may continue living as if she were alone; you might say she marches to the beat of her own drum. Younger

Sagittarians can be reckless, but as they mature, they can be drawn to religion, philosophy, and the occult.

Aries and Leo make the best matches, as Sagittarius is able to bend to Leo's ways, or at least pretend to. Sagittarians often end up with Aquarians, but their marriages do not tend to be for the long haul. They are attracted to Geminis, but are unlikely to marry one until middle age, when both signs have settled down. Sagittarius and Cancer have incredible sexual chemistry, but an actual relationship between them would be tumultuous and difficult. Capricorn can make a good partner- as long as they are able to respect each other's quirks. Sagittarius rarely ends up with a Virgo, and while she may often meet Pisces, things are unlikely to go very far.

CAPRICORN

Capricorn women are conscientious, reliable, organized, and hard-working. Many believe that life means nothing but work, and live accordingly. They are practical, and not particularly drawn to parties or loud groups of people. But if someone useful will be there, they are sure to make an appearance. Capricorn women are stingy, but not as much as their male counterparts. They are critical of others, but think highly of themselves. Generally, they take a difficult path in life, but thanks to their dedication, perseverance, and willingness to push their own limits, they are able to forge their own path, and by 45 or 50, they can provide themselves with anything they could want. Capricorn women have the peculiarity of looking older than their peers when they are young, and younger than everyone else once they have matured. They are not particularly sexual, and tend to be faithful partners. They rarely divorce, and even will fight until the end, even for a failed marriage. Many Capricorns have a pessimistic outlook of life, and have a tendency to be depressed. They are rarely at the center of any social circle, but are excellent organizers. They have a very rigid view of life and love, and are not interested in a fling, as marriage is the end goal. As a wife, Capricorn is simultaneously difficult and reliable. She is difficult because of her strict nature and difficulty adapting. But she will also take on all the household duties, and her husband can relax, knowing his children are in good hands.

Taurus, Pisces, and Scorpio make good matches. Aries is difficult, once things cool off after the initial honeymoon. When a Capricorn meets another Capricorn, they will be each other's first and last love. Sagittarius isn't a bad match, but they don't always pass the test of time. Aquarius and Capricorn are a difficult match, and rarely found together. Things are too dull with a Virgo, and while Leo can be exciting at first, things will fall apart when he begins showing off. Libra and Aquarius are both difficult partners for Capricorn, and she is rarely found with either of them.

AQUARIUS

A female Aquarius is very different from her male counterparts. She is calm and keeps a cool head, but she is also affectionate and open. She values loyalty above all else, and is unlikely to recover from any infidelity, though she will only divorce if this becomes a chronic trend, and she has truly been stabbed in the back. She is not interested in her partner's money, but rather, his professional success. She is unobtrusive and trusting, and will refrain from listening in on her partner's phone conversations or hacking into his email. With rare exceptions, Aquarian women make terrible housewives. But they are excellent partners in life – they are faithful, never boring, and will not reject a man, even in the most difficult circumstances. Most Aquarians are highly intuitive, and can easily tell the truth from a lie. They themselves only lie in extreme situations, which call for a "white lie" in order to avoid hurting someone's feelings.

Aquarius gets along well with Aries, Gemini, and Libra. She can also have a good relationship with a Sagittarius. Taurus often makes a successful match, though they are emotionally very different; the same goes for Virgo. Aquarius and Scorpio, Capricorn, or Cancer is a difficult match. Pisces can make a good partner as well, as both signs complement each other. Any relationship with a Leo will be tumultuous, but lasting, as Leo is selfish, and Aquarius will therefore have to be very forgiving.

PISCES

Pisces women are very adaptable, musically inclined, and erotic. They possess an innate earthly wisdom, and a good business sense. Pisces often reinvent themselves; they can be emotional, soft, and obstinate, as well as sentimental, at times. Their behavioral changes can be explained by frequent ups and downs. Pisces is charming, caring, and her outward malleability is very attractive to men. She is capable of loving selflessly, as long as the man has something to love. Even if he doesn't, she will try and take care of him until the very end. Pisces' greatest fear is poverty. They are intuitive, vulnerable, and always try to avoid conflict. They love to embellish the truth, and sometimes alcohol helps with this. Rarely, one finds extremely unbalanced, neurotic and dishonest Pisces, who are capable of turning their loved ones' lives into a living Hell!

Taurus, Capricorn, Cancer, and Scorpio make the best matches. She will be greatly attracted to a Virgo, but a lasting relationship is only likely if both partners are highly spiritual. Any union with a Libra is likely to be difficult and full of conflict. Pisces finds Gemini attractive, and they may have a very lively relationship – for a while. Occasionally, Pisces ends up with a Sagittarius, but she will have to fade into the background and entirely submit to him. If she ends up with an Aquarius, expect strong emotional outbursts, and a marriage that revolves around the need to raise their children.

Tatiana Borsch

Manufactured by Amazon.ca
Bolton, ON